Grace
— TO —
PRAY

"In all things grace abounds."

Written by

Diane M. Henderson

Photo Design Credit: Milan Williams

PREFACE

Greetings Beloved and to the Faithful in Christ

I am so excited about what God is doing with His people in this season. I am a strong advocate for God's bride becoming a House of Prayer. It is also true that every great revival and awakening period began with a season of diligent, fervent prayer. Personally, I believe it is the absolute will of God to strengthen and equip you to stand in the gap and make up the hedge. If prayer has been a struggle for you, cheer up and be encouraged because things are about to *shift* as God draws you into His secret place. My prayer is that every stumbling block and distraction assigned to hinder your prayer life will be rooted out. Furthermore, I have prayed for you beloved, that God will break into your hearts with a "spirit of burning" that will not be quenched.

Trust and believe that God is about to do a new thing in your life and you will never be the same. Indeed, the former things will pass away and all things will become new. Moreover, I decree abundant grace is resting upon you to pray without ceasing and see many people touched and impacted because of your intercession. So please do not put this book down or dismiss what God has to say about one of the most important topics on His heart. Make a radical effort to press in and grab hold to the grace that has been imparted to you by embracing these principles of prayer. Child of God, right now, I hear a word of encouragement for you. Listen carefully as the Spirit of Grace whispers the mind of the Lord.

"My son, my daughter stay focused now, for indeed this is a new season and purpose to become steadfast in prayer. I am looking for the one who will be faithful to call upon me. Beloved, I have anointed you and chosen you for such a time as this. This is the time for you to step out in grace and faith and use the anointing to break the power of the enemy off your family members and off my people. There are still too many who do not know me and are being held back by the powers and principalities of this present world. But even as I called Peter to be a fisher of men, so I have chosen you and anointed you to go forth, pulling many out of the fire-- for indeed, the harvest is ready. As you abide in me, lean not to your own understanding, but have faith in me; I will gird you up and show you how to use the anointing to set the captives free, to heal the sick and break open the heavens and declare my will for the earth. Be bold now and strong in faith. Say not that I am only a man; but, I say to you trust me to use you and send you forth. You are ready for any challenge, and I have equipped you by giving you an overcoming spirit and the heart of a warrior. So arise in new

strength and faith to fulfill the mandate and destiny you were created for."

DEDICATION

This book is dedicated, first and foremost, to my family. The power of prayer has worked so wonderfully in our lives to bring many changes and breakthroughs.

In addition, this book is dedicated to every prayer warrior and believer who wants to rise to the next level of prayer. May God grace you to pray always.

ACKNOWLEDGEMENTS

I honor the Holy Spirit who has been patient with me and who guides me in all things.

I would like to thank Brother Anthony Hill and Sister Tammy Johnson for assisting me with the editing process. In addition, I would like to thank Lakeisha Bolling for the prayers and encouraging words.

I would like to give a special thanks to Sherry N. King and Sherry King International Enterprises for inspiring me to strive for a spirit of excellence. Her patience, creativity and insight have been a great blessing in taking this book to a new level.

Also, I would like to thank Bishop Kyle and Pastor Kemi Searcy for leading the way.

Thank you to the reader for getting a copy of this book. Please pass it on.

TABLE OF CONTENTS

Grace to Pray: A Personal Revelation

Hebrews 4:16 invites believers to come boldly to the throne of grace that they may obtain mercy and find grace to help in time of need. God's wrath will be released against those who oppose Him; but for now, He invites us to come without fear or timidity. God is so willing to come to our aid, but we have to be willing and obedient to receive His invitation. It is very encouraging to know it is not always sin and disobedience that leads us to the throne of grace. Hebrews tells us it is to obtain mercy and find help in a time of need. This invitation to come should be very comforting because we all need assurance of His grace and mercy from time to time. The goodness and kindness of the Lord cannot be disregarded on this side of heaven!

A few months ago, in a dream, I was talking to a woman about prayer. In the dream she asked, "How did you learn to pray all the time?" I humbly, but with confidence replied, *"God has given me grace to pray."* I believe God used this dream to give me tremendous insight that it is indeed God's grace that enables believers to pray without ceasing (1 Thessalonians 5:17). It can be said that often times believers lack a genuine understanding of how to pray. The scriptures declare, "Likewise the Spirit also helpeth our infirmities: for we know now what we should pray for as we ought: but the Spirit itself maketh intercession for us with groaning which cannot be uttered" (Romans 8:26). Even the disciples who followed Jesus knew there was something very different about the way our Lord prayed and inquired to know more about it. Perhaps after they overheard the Master praying early one morning, as He was accustomed to do, they knew it was only the Lord who could teach them to pray. A brief account of the Lord's answer and prayer is recorded in the book of Luke 11:1 *"And it came to pass, that, as He was praying in a certain place, when He ceased, one of His disciples said unto Him, Lord, teach us to pray, as John also taught his disciples."*

When you hear a real child of God praying or just talking to God about what is on their heart, there is something very attractive about it. It is difficult to explain or define, but there is something about prayer that is so wonderful and heartfelt that you must pursue it for yourself. This was my experience when I first began to pray. I admit that I was full of envy as I heard the more seasoned saints intercede. I did not know the language and had not yet memorized any familiar scriptures on prayer, but to my surprise, as I began to hang around the elders and intercessors, I learned how to commune with God. I was also falling in love with Jesus and becoming more intimate with a person who was so precious to me. I learned that by experience, He is not only my God and Creator; He is our Abba Papa who loves us dearly and has paid the ultimate price by sending his only Son. The quest to know God and be close to Him strengthened my resolve to learn His heart and to become a student of the Word. I admonish you (the reader) to spend time chasing after God so you may lay a good foundation that will strengthen your walk with Christ for many years. It is a tremendous blessing to be highly favored by God. John 15:16 declares, *"Ye have not chosen me, but I have chosen you, and ordained you, that ye should go forth and bring forth fruit, and that your fruit should remain: that whatsoever ye shall ask of the Father in my name, he may give it you."* This is a great joy! I concur with the words of a fellow Intercessor who said, "You can do more than pray after you have prayed, but you cannot do more than pray until you have prayed." --A.J. Gordon.

What is Grace?

In one of his sermons, Bishop Kyle Searcy, Senior Pastor of Fresh Anointing House of Worship in Montgomery, Alabama shared an acronym for the word "GRACE." Bishop Searcy stated the word grace could be defined as "**G**od's **R**iches **A**t **C**hrist's **E**xpense." There is a lot of truth in that statement, and I believe the Holy Spirit inspired such a thought. A lot can be said about **grace** and what it means in the life of a believer. Paul, the great Apostle who persecuted the people of God, had his own revelation of grace when he said, *"But by the grace of God I am what I am: and his grace which was bestowed upon me was not in vain; but I labored more abundantly than they all; yet not I, but the grace of God which was with me"* (1 Corinthians 15:10). The great Apostle Paul acknowledged that it was only by grace that his laboring was not in vain. He counted his call to the ministry a great joy that he should preach among the Gentiles the unsearchable riches of Christ.

In addition, most of the letters of the Apostle Paul such as Ephesians, Romans, and Galatians begin with a greeting that reads something like this, *"Grace be unto you, and peace, from God our Father, and from the Lord Jesus Christ"* (1 Corinthians 1:3). You will find this same greeting time after time as Paul addresses the various churches in his letters. Nobody understood the grace of God more than the Apostle Paul, who said he was a blasphemer and a persecutor, but he obtained mercy from the Lord because he did it out of ignorance and unbelief. If anyone was not worthy to be used by God and called to the ministry, it would be Saul who was later called Paul. Remember this beloved, as God transforms our lives, we cannot stay the same. We will be changed from glory to glory until we come into the fullness of Christ. I can emphatically say that the heart of God is redemptive when it comes to the salvation of mankind. After all, the greatest sacrifice of God showing us his love came when God sent his son to die for us. As the scriptures tell us in Ephesians 2:4, *"But God who is rich in mercy, for his great love wherewith he loved us."* Paul was forgiven and counted faithful as God so beautifully transformed his life and called him into the ministry. Let us stop for a moment to examine a wonderful but complex thing we call grace and why so many believers stumble in applying God's grace when it is so abundant to us all.

In his article, "What is Grace?" author Lonnie Kent York expounds on its meaning. York says, "The most common understanding of the word *"grace"* is the unmerited favor and love of God toward man." We all can accept this simple, yet concise definition. York makes several references to the word *grace* as he continues by saying, "The grace of God is the time that God has shed forth all of His mercy and extended to us a period of time, by which we have opportunity to redeem ourselves from our sins" (p. 2). This definition gives us an understanding of grace that would be hard to misinterpret as a license to sin. In other words, shall we continue to sin repeatedly, because we have a perverted concept of the very reason we should not sin? The Apostle Peter warned the Church when he declared there were false prophets among the people and false teachers who would bring in damnable heresies, even denying the Lord, bringing destruction on themselves and others (see 2 Peter 1). I declare to you that we are living in such a time as the end of days draw near. Even now, there are false teachers and false prophets in the Church today perverting the Gospel and having an anti-Christ spirit. May the Holy Spirit who is our helper deliver us from deception and every false way that would cause us not to follow Christ.

Regardless of how one may understand or define God's grace, every believer needs to access that grace so we may fulfil our prophetic destiny. Apart from the work of grace in our lives, we would all fall utterly short. What a glorious God who has redeemed us by the blood of his Son and not by our own works. Selah! The same grace that enabled Paul time after time is still accessible to us.

The book of Acts tells us God poured out *great grace* upon the early Church as they were being established in the faith and moving forward in Kingdom purposes. The greatest act of grace poured out by God came when He sent His Son to redeem us from the curse of the law. This same grace is upon the present Church and every believer has access to it. Moreover, this grace is still abundant in cultivating a lifestyle of prayer and intercession. Children of God, it is free for the asking and we can have all the grace we need. For the heavens are open.

To further expound on the necessity of depending on God's grace, I am thoroughly convinced that there is **grace to pray** all the time." One of my favorite scriptures declares, *"And God is able to make all grace abound toward you; that ye, always having all sufficiency in all things, may abound to every good work"* (2 Corinthians 9:8). To know and receive God's grace is a wonderful thing because it cost God the life of His Son. May the Lord who is rich in mercy help each and every one of us to receive what we could never earn and do not deserve.

Reflection and Review: It is me- it's me oh Lord, standing in the need of grace.

1. How has the grace of God worked in your own life? Give examples:

2. What are some of the benefits of resting in God's grace?

3. Do you believe the grace of God can see you through any situation? Explain.

CHAPTER ONE

Defining Prayer: Keeping it Simple

A simple and basic definition of prayer is "talking to God." Mike Bickle's revelation of prayer goes something like this: "All prayer- is asking God to tell you what to tell Him." I think that is a pretty good revelation on prayer. Bickle, the founder of International House of Prayer (IHOP) in Kansas City, gives further insight into a more complex definition of prayer as he asks the question, *"What is prayer? It is talking to God. It is at the same time a great privilege, a fierce struggle, and a powerful miracle of the Spirit who helps us in our weakness in prayer."*

There is no need to complicate what prayer is by defining it with big words. It is vanity if all we do is define prayer, acquaint ourselves with scriptures on prayer, and still neglect to spend time in prayer. However, I do believe, as we mature in our relationship with the Lord and grow in faith the many components of prayer may take on a deeper more profound meaning. Think about a one-year old. At this age, his vocabulary and cognitive development are very limited; but to the child's advantage, his wise and loving parents will not only provide for him, they will love him unconditionally. At four- or five-years of age, this same infant should have a much more extended vocabulary and a greater ability to articulate his needs and desires. It is the same way with our spiritual development. *As newborn babes, we should desire the sincere milk of the word that we may grow thereby (1 Peter 2:2).*

Prayer for a believer should be as natural as the process of children developing their ability to communicate and express their thoughts more clearly. We should make great effort to grow in relational intimacy with the Lord by communing with the Holy Spirit on a daily basis. I believe the foundation for all true prayer is birthed out of relational intimacy. That means having a pure heart and a passionate love for the Bridegroom. As we become acquainted with the great Intercessor and learn about Him, prayer becomes easier and our daily walk becomes a delight. Psalm 34:8 puts it well, *"Oh taste and see that the Lord is good: blessed is the man that trusteth in him."*

There is an Old Testament passage that states, "He made known His ways unto Moses, His acts unto the children of Israel" (Psalms 103:7). As dear children, we not only want greater clarity of what God is doing and saying, but we should experience the reality of knowing who He is. As we grow in "sonship," we begin to understand His nature, character and attributes. His word tells us He reveals His secrets to His friends. There is an Old Testament character in the book of Genesis by the name of E'noch who enjoyed his fellowship with the Lord. E'noch and God were so intimate that God just took him to Heaven one day as they went for their daily stroll. They had such a connection with each other that God said today is your day you are coming home with me. We also do well to remember this testimony that E'noch pleased God. It is quite evident that being a friend of God will go a long way in helping us become people of prayer. In other words, let us not just know prayer - let's do prayer. Like the woman in Luke 18 who was persistent in going before the judge so her request would not be denied, we too must persist in faithfulness to prayer.

"Seven days without prayer makes one weak." --*Allen Vartlett*

There is a lot to be said about prayer. It would probably take the span of a lifetime to learn only a small portion of what it truly means to "pray without ceasing." Prayer for a believer can be likened to what water is to fish and oxygen is to breathing. We just cannot live without it! Forget all that deep stuff and prayer terminology that keeps tripping us up. We know too much already and that may be half the problem. Knowing what to do and not doing it is worse than not knowing at all. There is an old saying that states, "Don't fix the wheel if it isn't broken." However, if the wheel is broken, how do we fix what is broken? So the wheel can be used effectively and get us where we need to go. Romans 8:26 puts it this way, *"Likewise the Spirit also helpeth our infirmities: for we know not what we should pray for as we ought: but the Spirit itself maketh intercession for us with groanings which cannot be uttered."* I remember once going to the Lord in prayer about a certain situation I was struggling with in life. I was consumed by what was going on in my life; but it did resonate to me, that my concern was not on the heart of God. However, as I drew near to the Lord in prayer I sensed the Lord saying, "That's not what I want you to pray right now, I've already taken care of it. I was somewhat surprised, but I remembered whose I was and began to pray as the Spirit led.

That was a good lesson for me as God revealed to me his will in prayer. Since that time, I have been sensitive to ask what is on the Father's heart to pray.

Much has already been written about prayer and yet it remains true that daily, consistent prayer and time with God may be the least followed disciplines for people who profess followers of Christ. This may be a hard pill to swallow for some of us; nevertheless, it is still true. It would not be expedient to mention the vast number of men and women, biblical and non-biblical, to validate the veracity of prayer and its power in the lives of people who have put their faith in God. As men and women of faith, we should have an understanding and expectation that God hears and answers prayer. As children of the Kingdom, we must press in for more and at the same time hear the words of God, *"Be still, and know that I am God"* (Psalm 46:10).

Prayer is a crucial and fundamental tool for the Church to fulfill her end-time mandate. Jesus said, *"It is written, My House shall be called a House of Prayer"* (Matthew 21:13). This wonderful, amazing grace for prayer will continue until Jesus comes. Is it not good to know the Son of God, our Great Intercessor, is still in a posture of prayer? Hebrews tells us, *"It is Christ that died, yea rather that is risen again, who is even at the right hand of God, who also maketh intercession for us"* (Romans 8:34).

We, the Christian church, have not lived up to the mandate of prayer given to us by the Lord. Perhaps this is why so many of God's people are spiritually anemic and suffer many things from the enemy. Many lack the power to resist the devil and fight the good fight of faith. The sixth chapter of Ephesians tells us to put on the whole armour of God that we may be able to stand against the wiles of the devil because our fight is not with flesh and blood. This exhortation to prayer may be summarized as Paul admonishes, *"...praying always with all prayer and supplication in the Spirit, and watching thereunto with all perseverance and supplication for all saints"* (Ephesians 6:18). People of God, we must be anxious for nothing. But in everything, by prayer, make our request known (Philippians 4:6, paraphrased). God is waiting on His Bride. Let us run to Him in our hour of need. Do you hear what the Spirit is saying to the Church? Do you know what time it is?

E.M. Bounds, a great author and man of prayer said, **"God shapes the world by prayer. The more praying there is in the world, the better the world will be and the mightier the forces against evil. God continues His cause and purpose of life on earth through the eternal value of prayer."**

As you read, ask yourself these questions. Are you committed to being a person of prayer or do you press into God with prayer in your time of distress? What sends you to the prayer closet or puts you on your knees? If you do not have clarity to these questions, keep reading and hang on. By the time you finish this book, the **spirit of prayer** will burn in your heart like nothing you have ever experienced. The Holy Spirit will train your hands to war and teach your fingers to fight. Believe me, child of God, not many days from now your prayer life will be turned upside down and what you did not have the grace to do in times past will be imparted to you and transform you into a mighty soldier of the cross.

Personal Testimony: I would like to share a little bit of my story. I was saved in the late eighties. Here I was newly married and had two small children to raise. I was a timid person in many respects and did not know how to pray. During those precious earlier years, God taught me how to hear His voice and receive His unconditional love. There was nothing I desired more than "to know God intimately." For hours upon hours, I would sit in His presence and devour His word as the Lord took me from Genesis to Revelation. I will always appreciate what God did for me as I waited on Him and sat at His feet. He was giving me a deep love for Him that would never be shaken. This was also a time when Holy Spirit taught me how to worship and sing songs out of my spirit. This was a most enjoyable season for me as the enabling grace of God strengthened me in every area.

You may experience times when the enemy will come up against you hard as you determine to pray. Do not ever give up. Do not ever throw in the towel. Hold steadfastly to God. Know that He is your Lord and friend. Without a doubt, I can say that praying, fasting and waiting on God will pay off. God consistently proves His faithfulness. I am a strong witness of the power of prayer in the life of a believer. Over the years, I have prayed hundreds and hundreds of prayers for others and myself, which God has answered. He may not always answer the way I expect Him to or according to my timetable, but God has never disappointed me. I believe when we are able to cultivate a lifestyle of prayer it will become our lifeline and serve as a great teaching tool in learning life lessons.

Chapter One: Questions for Reflection

1. How often do you pray? Write a brief paragraph.

2. What things do you most pray about? Relational issues, finances, health problems, other?

3. What are some of steps you can take for your prayer life to grow?

CHAPTER TWO

What Makes Prayer Work?

From Genesis to Revelation the call to prayer is undeniable as ELOHIM, Creator of all things, makes this profound decree: *"Call unto me, and I will answer thee, and show thee great and mighty things which thou knowest not"* (Jeremiah 33:3). Furthermore, Genesis 4:26 states, *"And to Seth, to him also there was born a son; and he called his name E'nos: then began men to call upon the name of the Lord."* There are some things that are in the sovereign will of God, such as the time of His return. But concerning the affairs of men, it is the will of God that men should seek him and pursue him that we might know him and be found of

27

him. It is an amazing thing in itself that the same God who created the sun, moon and stars would still take the time to be mindful of us. The Old and New Testaments confirm and validate the necessity of prayer with men and women chosen to do his will. From Abraham to Moses and from the disciples to the Apostle Paul, anyone who was converted by the grace message became a person of prayer. You cannot do the work of God aside from spending time in prayer. Again, there is no way a believer can successfully fulfill his call to Christ without knowing the necessity of prayer. Spending time with God and knowing his ways is necessary for us to pray the heart of God for words alone are not enough. The scripture tells us *"He made known his ways unto Moses, his acts unto the children of Israel"* (Psalms 103:7). It is the heart and spirit of a thing that is needed as we fellowship and commune with God, Spirit to spirit.

Why is prayer so hard?

So, here is the million-dollar question. Why is cultivating a lifestyle of prayer so hard for many of God's people?

It is true that many of God's children want to pray more than they do, but consistency in prayer seems to **elude** them. How do we get a true understanding of the responsibility of man, which is doing our part versus allowing the Holy Spirit to do his part? Well, I believe that if we get a true revelation of the *grace of God*, any doubleminded thinking would be resolved. Maybe there is not a single answer to this ongoing problem that has been plaguing the body of Christ for so long. Maybe it is only for the intercessors and true prayer warriors. Maybe God did not mean his people are to pray without ceasing. Nevertheless, if we believe the scriptures we know that every promise from God is "yes" and "amen." If we call upon this God to help us, He will answer indeed. As we examine the New Testament, let us look at Jesus, the perfect model for developing a consistent lifestyle of prayer. What do we see in his relationship with the Father? Did he take prayer seriously? I can say with a degree of confidence, the last words spoken by a dying man to have great value. Some of the last words uttered by the Lord was in this prayer, *"Father, forgive them; for they know not what they do."* Luke 23:34 states, *"But now that the Master is dead what do we do?"* Jesus knew He only had a short time to finish His work, but He promised to send back the Holy Spirit who would comfort us and guide us into all truth.

As the scriptures tell us, Jesus' disciples were given clear instructions not to depart from Jerusalem but to wait for the promise. That promise was the gift of the Holy Spirit. The Lord spoke with the disciples many times of His suffering and death. Jesus knew the concept of His departure would be a hard thing for the men who followed Him to bear, so He promised them He would not leave them comfortless.

The Master assured his followers that it was more expedient that He go away, so He could send back a Helper who would teach them all things. When the Lord ascended back to the Father, their hearts were saddened as they quickly forgot the promise he had spoken to them. Luke 24 gives us a clear description of how they felt as they drew near to the village called Emmaus.

And, behold two of them went that same day to a village called Emmaus, which was from Jerusalem about threescore furlongs. And they talked together of all these things which had happened. And it came to pass, that, while they communed together and reasoned, Jesus himself drew near, and went with them. But their eyes were holden that they should not know him. And he said unto them, What manner of communications are these that ye have one to another as ye walk, and are sad? Luke 24:13-17.

It is obvious that they had forgotten the words and the promises of the Lord only a few weeks before his death. Although the Lord drew near to them, He did not immediately reveal Himself, but He reminded them of what the prophets and the scriptures taught. *"Then He said unto them, O fools, and slow of heart to believe all that the Prophets have spoken: Ought not Christ to have suffered these things, and to enter into his glory?"* Jesus rebuked them for their unbelief. Nevertheless, the weighty words of our Lord opened their eyes and they returned to Jerusalem encouraged, saying "the Lord has risen indeed." If only the disciples could see, the best was yet to come. Before his death, Jesus had commanded them that they should not depart from Jerusalem, but wait for the promise of the father, which sayeth He, *"Ye have heard of me"* (Acts 1:4). Suddenly, it was time to put what they had learned into action. As the disciples, along with the women, tarried in the upper room with one accord in prayers and supplications, the understanding of what Jesus had promised was fulfilled and their joy was full.

Jesus ascended back to the Father, but he did not leave them without a Comforter. This time they would not doubt Him or fall back to their old ways. They would embrace a supernatural enablement for their prayers to be effective and on the day of Pentecost, the Holy Spirit showed up and filled each one with power. The promise spoken by the Prophet Joel was now fulfilled. God poured out his Spirit. Suddenly, the disciples had power to be His witnesses and to pray for hours as the men and women gathered into the upper room (Acts 1:14).

Jesus is faithful to His word. He gave His followers supernatural power to pray by filling them with the Holy Spirit. This divine enablement would also help them to overcome the enemy as they moved forward to do the work of the ministry. The early church was birthed through ordinary men and women who believed in the power of prayer. It is still the Holy Spirit who teaches us to pray. Not by might or by power, can we live a lifestyle of prayer. It is not a work of the flesh. It is only by His Spirit.

Jesus, the Son of God, modeled a lifestyle of prayer and boldly stated, *"I can of mine self do nothing: as I hear, I judge: and my judgment is just; because I seek not mine own will, but the will of the Father which hath sent me"* (John 5:30). Jesus stated time and time again that He was only doing what the Father told Him to do and this included a model of prayer.

One of my favorite passages on Jesus instructing us how to pray is shown in Matthew 6. Beginning in the sixth chapter of Matthew he says, *"And when thou prayest, thou shall not be as the hypocrites are; for they love to pray standing in the synagogues and in the corners of the streets, that they may be seen of men. Verily I say unto you, they have their reward. But when ye pray, use not vain repetitions, as the heathen do, for they think that they shall be heard for their much speaking."*

No doubt, Jesus had observed the religious prayers of the scribes and the Pharisees. Jesus understood the true essence of prayer, which is born out of relationship and communion with the Father. In these passages, He gave several key secrets to building a successful prayer life. Let me simplify what I believe He is saying.

a. Do not pray to be seen or heard by men: God hates hypocrisy and pretention.

b. Pray to your Father in secret and shut the door: Personal prayer alone with God is vital.

c. Do not use vain repetitions in your prayers. Do not keep saying the same thing. Ask yourself this: If I were talking to a good friend right now, would I speak to him/her like this. Tell the Father what you need and expect Him to answer.

d. Jesus concludes His model of prayer by telling us to forgive our debtors even as we want to be forgiven for our debts. When we forgive others and release them from their offenses the enemy no longer has an open door to come in.

The Lord hates pride and pretense as He addressed the religious people of His day that appeared to be righteous. Jesus discerned that the motives of their hearts were full of hypocrisy and He gives a harsh rebuke to the religious people of His day. He also gives a vivid description of the conditions of their hearts and how their own rituals and ungodly deeds were an abomination to Him. In the following verse, the Lord's observation of what was going on goes something like this, *"Woe unto you, scribes and Pharisees, hypocrites! For ye make clean the outside of the cup and of the platter, but within they are full of extortion and excess. Thou blind Pharisee, cleanse first that which is within the cup and platter that the outside of them may be clean also. Woe unto you, scribes and Pharisees, hypocrites! Even so ye also outwardly appear righteous unto men, but within ye are full of hypocrisy and iniquity"* Matthew 23:25-28.

No child of God can read Matthew 23 without understanding how much the Lord hates hypocrisy. Beloved, either we are in or we are out. We are either for Him or against Him. Darkness cannot be light and light cannot be darkness. We cannot say good is evil or call evil good. Either we belong to Him and His Spirit abides within us or He will say to us go away from me. "I never knew you." Brethren, the call to prayer cannot be denied. The mandate on God's people is that we become a House of Prayer. So what is the final conclusion of the matter? The Holy Spirit will teach us how to pray and the grace that God provides is without measure.

Finally, God is a righteous judge and He will not make a demand for us to do anything that He has not empowered us to do. We have not, because we ask not. Let us ask and expect to receive. It is our portion.

Chapter Two: Questions for Reflection

1. What are some of the stumbling blocks you must overcome to go higher in prayer?

2. Has your journey of prayer been a difficult one? Explain.

3. Write out at least one thing you can do to remain consistent in prayer.

CHAPTER THREE

Why Pray?

Jesus not only taught the disciples how to pray, but He Himself is the very model of what prayer should look like. Scripture tells us that He was often found in prayer, as He was accustomed to do. *"And when He had sent the multitudes away, He went up into a mountain apart to pray: and when the evening was come, He was there alone"* (Matthew 14:23). It is an awesome thing to know the Son of God was committed to prayer. He made the statement, *"Verily, verily I say unto you, The Son can do nothing of himself, but what he seeth the Father do: for what things so ever he doeth, these also doeth the Son likewise"* (John 5:19). Jesus did not assume to do anything on his own, but committed all things to the Father in prayer. There are many examples in the scripture that confirm our Lord's devotion to prayer. Jesus affirms, *"It is written my house shall be called a House of Prayer..."* (Matthew 21:13).

Jesus told us when we pray to believe, we will receive the things we have prayed. Prayer is a basic fundamental right of the Christian faith. Jesus expects us to spend time in prayer. Since He is the epitome of prayer, we should have the same standard and level of accountability by learning how to become people of prayer and intercession. It is evident the ministry of intercession still holds a high place in the life of Jesus. His Word tells us that He is at the right hand of God and continues to make intercession for us. Wow! That will give you something to chew on. Selah. People of God, we cannot live the Christian life or walk in victory without practicing the art of prayer. The great reformer Martin Luther made this statement: "To be a Christian without prayer is no more possible than to be alive without breathing." Listed below are just a few reasons why we must pray. Let us examine a few of them as we move forward.

1. We have an enemy – that is why we must pray!

This adversary known as Satan opposed God by leading a revolt in Heaven that caused at least one third of the angels to fall. Satan and his hord of demons continue to hinder and oppose those who are followers of Christ. We must know that Satan comes to steal, kill and destroy. The devil is the god of this world and he has blinded the eyes of many to keep them from believing the truth and the person of truth. He hinders multitudes, even nations, from coming to Christ through deception and spiritual blindness. The evil one holds people in captivity through a spirit of bondage, unbelief and idolatry. Sadly, the greatest battlefield is still in the mind. The scriptures declare, *"But if our Gospel be hid, it is hid to them that are lost. In whom the god of this world has blinded the minds of them which believe not, lest the light of the glorious gospel of Christ, who is the image of God, should shine unto them"* (2 Corinthians 4:3-4).

As we learn to change our thinking patterns and paradigms, we will embrace victory in so many ways. Little children, our fight is not with flesh and blood, but against principalities, powers, rulers of the darkness of this world and wickedness in high places. If the Church ever gets a revelation of how to fight the good fight of faith, we will have an awesome victory on this side of heaven. It is true that prayer, intercession and learning how to travail in the Spirit will break many yokes and bring down many strongholds. We cannot put every trouble or affliction we have on the devil, but we can learn to discern true spiritual warfare and deal with it in an effective way. (See the book of Job).

2. Another reason we must pray is so we can learn to live out of the spirit.

Most Evangelical Christians believe the Godhead consist of three Gods in one. That is God the Father, God the Son (Jesus) and God the Holy Spirit. We refer to this as the Trinity. As human beings, we are made of three parts: we are spirit- that part that relates to God, our soul-which is made of the mind, will and emotions, and our bodies-which is our earthly tabernacle. **For scriptures tell us we groan earnestly desiring to be clothed upon** with our true house which is from heaven (2 Corinthians).

When we give Jesus, lordship of our lives, His spirit joins with our spirit and we become one with God. At the point of conversion, we are only newborn babes on the milk of the Word. Our sins have been forgiven and Jesus washes us in His blood. However, it will still take much work, time and prayer to learn how to live out of our spirit and not the flesh or the carnal man. You are quite familiar with the old man that has been running your life and telling you what to do. Now you have been awakened to the new man in Christ who will guide you and instruct you in the ways of the spirit. You must learn not to be conformed or shaped by this world and its systems, but become transformed by the renewing of your minds.

As Romans 12:1 indicates, we must present our bodies a living sacrifice, holy and acceptable unto God, which is our reasonable service. The great Apostle Paul said, *"I die daily."* Paul believed and instructed those who would follow Christ to, continually, mortify the deeds of the flesh. He expounds on this awesome struggle between flesh and spirit in Romans 7:8 by stating that the things he wanted to do he did not do and those things he did not wish to do he found himself doing. The antidote to this conflict is found in Romans 8:1, "There is no condemnation to those who walk in the Spirit and not after the flesh." Prayer helps us to mortify deeds of the flesh and walk in the Spirit.

3. **We must pray because souls are hanging in the balance.**

Our Lord Jesus has paid an awesome price for the souls of men. He left the streets of Glory and laid down his life for sinful man that we might spend eternity with Him. Spending time in prayer will sensitize our hearts and minds to the agony and burden that God feels for the lost. A beautiful example of God's heart for unbelievers is found in the book of Jonah. God sent Jonah to preach repentance to a nation that He would soon judge for its great wickedness. The story has a beautiful twist when the pagan king and his people believed what the prophet preached and repented. The people of Nineveh not only repented - they fasted, prayed, and humbled themselves before the God of the Hebrews. In response to their change of heart, God turned from His wrath and spared the people. As the Prophet Joel declares, *"Multitudes, multitudes in the valley of decision: for the day of the Lord is near in the valley of decision"* *(Joel 3:14)*. In every generation, there are multitudes of people who are in the valley of decision waiting for their hearts to be awakened to the fullness of what God has for them. May our hearts be stirred to go after them, even snatching them out of the fire if need be. Truly, the harvest is ready, but the laborers are still too few.

4. We must pray to keep our passion and relationship with the Lord fresh.

Beloved, how can we do the work of God and stay on track with Him if we have become lukewarm ourselves. It is easy to get caught up in serving God and just doing the work. Every believer needs those times of refreshing; that comes from being in the presence of the Lord. The daily cleansing and washing that comes from being in His presence and abiding at His feet. As we seek Him on a daily basis, we will not grow weary in well doing. Jesus had to confront the religious system enforced by men like the Pharisees and Sadducees who had succumbed to a set of rules and regulations. They gave Him lip service, but their hearts were far from Him. Consequently, their ignorance of God and his word made their work of none affect. God is all about transforming the lives of his people. As we grow in our relationship and give Him, our hearts the call to do His work will graciously flow out of us.

There are numerous passages in the word that admonish us to pray in both the Old and New Testaments. The word of God gives us many people who were great examples of why prayer is so necessary. One of my favorite passages on prayer is found in 2 Chronicles 7:14 which says, *"If my people which are called by my name, shall humble themselves, and pray, and seek my face, and turn from their wicked ways: then will I hear from heaven, and will forgive their sin, and will heal their land."* Prayer is still one of the major tenants of the Christian faith. True, fervent and passionate prayer can be powerful and bring great victories that will not happen if we do not pray. When I think of the countless prayers, I have prayed in my walk with God, it would be impossible to name them all. Yet I have not failed to see the goodness of God in answering prayers to this day. **Remember beloved the only prayer that is not answered is the one you do not pray!** True prayer still moves the hand of God **(His power)** and the heart of God **(His love and compassion)**, so we may know that He is God and all things are possible if we believe. So, Spirit of Burning Come!

5. So why pray? Because it must needs be!

Just as it was ordained for Jesus to go through Samaria and meet the woman at the well, the Body of Christ must become a House of Prayer. We have a saying around our Church that goes something like this, "Little prayer, little power; much prayer, much power." I concur with that statement and hopefully you agree with me.

God's word encourages us to pray without ceasing and Jesus speaks of a parable which says, *"Men ought always pray and not faint"* (Luke 18:1). This particular parable encourages us to stay before God and not give up because in due season our Lord will come with a righteous recompense. Child of God, now do you understand why praying is not an option for the believer? It is a dire necessity because the King's business requires haste! May we do our due diligence and remain faithful to the call of prayer.

"There is no power like that of prevailing prayer, of Abraham pleading for Sodom, Jacob wrestling in the stillness of the night. Moses standing in the breach, Hannah intoxicated with sorrow, David heartbroken with remorse and grief, Jesus in sweat of blood. Add to this list from the records of the church your personal observation and experience, and always there is the cost of passion unto blood. Such prayer prevails. It turns ordinary mortals into men of power. It brings power. It brings fire. It brings rain. It brings life. It brings God." --Samuel Chadwick

Chapter Three: Questions for Reflection

1. What are some of the reasons you must pray?

2. Are you motivated to help someone learn simple steps to prayer? Why or why not?

3. Among the reasons listed above to pray, which one ministered to you the most? Expound.

CHAPTER FOUR

Learning How to Pray

Now that we know some of the reasons we need to pray and how to access the grace to pray. How do we learn to pray? A lifestyle of prayer may be a learning process, but that does not mean it is complicated. We just have to hang in there and stay the course. Remember the analogy about the toddler who learns how to communicate with his parents. His first words may be mama and dada, but eventually his vocabulary will increase and he will learn to articulate and communicate with great skill. It is the same way in the Spirit. Understanding spiritual things does not happen overnight. None of us are born prayer warriors or become skilled in prayer without paying a price.

A daily discipline of time spent with the Lord will certainly enhance our ability and confidence in the prayer chamber. My introduction in learning how to pray was having a desire for it and simply hanging around the ones who were already praying. I assumed the pastor, elders and other seasoned members knew how to talk to God, and so I endeavored to imitate them. In my early walk with Christ, this proved to be very helpful. I was also faithful in attending weekly intercessory meeting with other believers. My prayer life became fruitful and my spirit became energized. I began to see results and answers to my prayers, repeatedly.

Listed below are a variety of ways we can grow and become skilled in prayer:

1. Hanging around mature seasoned people of prayer will greatly improve your prayer life.

We have a saying at my church that really drives the message home - prayer is more caught than taught. Taking that first step in learning how to pray may be as easy as hanging around those who pray. I learned so much about prayer by just being in the presence of men and women more seasoned and mature in prayer. It can be a little intimidating when you do not possess the skills of a prayer/intercessor, but stay the course. Holy Spirit is at work!

2. *Learning how to worship God and studying the Word will enhance your prayer life.*

As a young believer, I was addicted to worship and loved being in the presence of the Lord. The Lord would inspire me by giving me spontaneous songs that I would write down and share with others. In addition, I began to saturate my spirit with God's word. During this time, I spent countless hours feasting on the scriptures. The Psalms and the Proverbs were especially delightful to me as I became sensitive in learning how to hear the voice of God.

3. Reading books on prayer will help strengthen your prayer life.

After joining the ministry over twenty years ago, I connected with my overseers, Bishop Kyle and Kemi Searcy, who introduced me to warfare prayer. Beloved, there are times we need to combat the attacks of the enemy by discerning the spirits. Also, I was introduced to the concept of personal deliverance, which I believe is a great benefit to every believer. I have found this to be a fact, even after being saved and washed in the blood we all have stuff –excess baggage and areas in our lives that God needs to clean up. You may say, but is not the blood of Jesus enough? Yes, the blood still works! Remember it is your spirit man that is connected with God, for God is a Spirit. However, the soulish man, which is your mind, will, and emotions must be controlled by your spirit man, so that in all things you may glorify God. The Father did not leave us comfortless; He has given us a helper and a guide. Two books that will serve as useful tools to awaken your spirit to prayer are *"Lord, Teach My Hands to War"* by Pastor Kemi Searcy and Cindy Jacob's *"Possessing the Gates of the Enemy."*

4. Dreams and Visions

Another learning tool God used to help teach me to pray came through dreams and visions. I have been a dreamer from my childhood until now. Before I came to know the Lord, most of my dreams were dark, vague and brought great distress. The enemy also used these dark dreams to instill a stronghold of fear into my spirit. For example, I would repeatedly dream of someone trying to kill me or always about to be bit by a serpent. The dreams came in various forms, but always the same results. I was not saved, so I did not know how to bind up the enemy and cancel his assignment. A short time after I accepted Christ as my Lord and Saviour, God broke fear off me and I began to dream and have divine revelations about his will and experience a deeper place in prayer. The time I spent in prayer became more delightful and as I like to say, he reveals to redeem. Prophetic dreams can be very insightful in learning how to pray effectively against the plans and schemes of the enemy. Pay attention to your dreams! **God may be trying to tell you something.** God will often use dreams to communicate and reveal things to us. This applies to unbelievers as well (See Genesis 20).

5. Journaling your thoughts is a very good way of hearing from God.

When we write out our thoughts and prayers, we can go back and read about things we have prayed for and discover how wonderfully God has answered. This proved to be very therapeutic for me in troubling times, but it was also rewarding as I realized God had answered many of my prayers. I recommend that you keep a record or journal of your prayers, answers of how the Lord will give you history with God, and assurance of His faithfulness during trying times. Journaling may not always be an easy discipline, but it can prove to be rewarding over time if we stay focused.

6. Prayer is conversing with God.

Prayer is a training ground for ministry and greatly helps in our ability to hear the voice of God. It took many years of interacting with God to realize that prayer is not just a one-way conversation. In prayer, we talk to the Father and share what is on our heart, but we must learn how to "quiet our spirit" and listen to what God wants to speak to us. He does have something to say, and remember one word from God can shift you into destiny and change your life. Many times in my alone time with God, he would deal with me about issues of the heart. God would repeatedly tell me to guard my heart and walk in love. As I turned to him for grace and strength, I knew he would strengthen me for truly his grace is sufficient.

A good way to start the dialogue is to consider the acronym ACTS which stands for **A**doration, **C**onfession, **T**hanksgiving, and **S**upplication. *Adoration* is our praise, which expresses our love for God. Because, He is worthy of our love and honor for who he is and not just what He does for us. *Confession* openly addresses the imperfections in our lives to God, to ask for forgiveness and seek help to overcome those weak areas. *Thanksgiving* is different from adoration, in that, it expresses our gratitude for what he has done. *Supplication* simply means a petition or request. If you choose to follow this simple acronym in your time of worship, it will prove to be effective and life changing.

7. Being consistent and having a quiet time and place to pray will also enhance your intimacy with the Lord.

God is looking for a body of people who will just hang out with Him. God is a relational being and His heart is for us to know him. You must spend sufficient time with him. Like Mary, we just need to sit at his feet and receive the greater portion. My bathroom was my first quiet place. Later, I transitioned to the living room, where I still meet with God.

The place we choose is not of great importance, but that we do it. As people of prayer, we must learn to build an altar and meet God there.

8. Being committed to corporate prayer.

God's word says one will put a thousand to flight, and two put ten thousand to flight. Brethren, it is a beautiful thing when brethren come together in prayer. There is no greater joy than when we as God's people come together in love and unity. I believe demons will tremble and be put to flight when the children of God are on one accord pressing into Kingdom purposes. God said it best in 2 Chronicles 7:14, *"If my people which are called by my name shall humble themselves and pray, and seek my face, and turn from their wicked ways; then will I hear from heaven, and will forgive their sin, and will heal their land."*

Finally, God is looking for a people to partner with in prayer, so his will can be done on earth as it is in Heaven. God is sovereign and some things he will do just because he is God and it is a part of his eternal plan. For the most part, God responds to the prayers of his people. He says, *"Call upon me and I will answer thee and show thee great and mighty things we know not"* (Jeremiah 33:3). Multitudes of people will be lost and perish if God's people are not diligent in prayer. William Booth says, *"Work as if everything depended upon your work, and pray as if everything depended upon your prayer."* I have spent hundreds of hours in prayer with God's people because being a part of united prayer brings great joy and strength to the body. The scriptures tell us, "Iron sharpens iron." We not only get strength from God, we get strength from one another. Individual prayer is needful, but as God's people, we must become intentional whenever our leaders call for seasons of prayer. Many of our churches fail to make God's house a House of Prayer. Our cities and nations are in desperate need of prayer and intercession.

In conclusion, a great passage on the power of corporate prayer is found in the book of Acts 12:5 *"Peter therefore was kept in prison: but prayer was made without ceasing of the church unto God for him."* It was a trying time for the early church. James had been killed already and Peter was apprehended and put in prison. I believe the greatest days are ahead of us and miracles await us as God is prepared to release a host of Angels to deliver and to rescue. However, like the disciples in the garden, we sleep.

Chapter Four: Questions for Reflection

1. Right now, what is your greatest hindrance to prayer?

2. What are some of the principles you can begin that will empower your prayer life?

3. Have you taken this burden to the Lord?

CHAPTER FIVE

Who Will Teach Me to Pray and What are the Benefits?

The word of God makes it plain who will teach us how to pray. The men who walked closely with Jesus addressed the dilemma of who would teach them to pray hundreds of years ago. I can imagine their approach to Jesus on this matter was humble and reverent. This task of learning to pray was not a bother to the **Master** because He fully understood the necessity of prayer. Jesus knew He only had a short time with the men He had chosen and the multitudes that followed him.

Our Lord was very strategic in using every moment to teach his people the ways of the Kingdom. Scripture tells us, *"For we know not what we should pray for as we ought: but the Spirit itself maketh intercession for us with groaning which cannot be uttered"* (Romans 8:26). When we commit our lives to the Lord, He will take the responsibility of teaching us how to pray. We need only ask Him and avail ourselves of any opportunities that will help us to grow. Getting a prayer partner may also be a good way of being strengthened in prayer. Reading books on prayer and intercession, going to prayer conferences and just being consistent in daily prayer will prove to be very beneficial in growing in the grace of prayer. It may take some time before you may consider yourself to be a prayer warrior, but hang in there. **You cannot spend time with God and not see great results.** When God calls your name and gives you your assignment, you will be confident and ready. You will become His battle ax and learn to do much damage to the kingdom of Satan. Do what you can to equip yourself in prayer. Becoming familiar with the scriptures is necessary, as you learn the promises you can stand on to oppose the kingdom of darkness. God tells us to put Him in remembrance of His word. Finally, trust the One who said greater is he that is in me, than he that is in the world. The One who knows how to make perfect intercession lives in you, and he is absolutely ready to teach your hands to war and your fingers to fight!

"I would rather teach one man to pray than ten men to preach." J.H. Jowett

"Bless the Lord, O my soul, and forget not all his benefits" (Psalm 103:2). Do you know there are great benefits for anyone who obeys God? When we are hired on a job, we expect a salary; but along with being paid, we also expect certain benefits such as sick days, vacation time and so on. In addition, anyone who operates a vehicle is required by law to have car insurance in case there is an accident. Paying for that car insurance for months and sometimes years may not always be pleasant or seem beneficial; but if an accident occurs, we surely enjoy reaping the benefits. God has many benefits for his children and these benefits may be obtained through prayer. He says, *"Ask and it shall be given, knock and the door will be opened, seek and ye shall find"* (Mathew 7:7). The Lord goes on to say, "For everyone who asks receives." What a wonderful promise we have from the Father, and there are many additional promises God gives to his children. There may be times, however, that the blessings are contingent upon our obedience and level of faith. This book would be exhausted if we tried to look at every single blessing and benefit attached to prayer. However, we can list a few things that will bring insight and understanding to the numerous benefits of prayer.

1. One of the greatest blessings to prayer is getting to know God.

The world tells us that we will know him even as we are known of Him. God wants a people who will walk with him and know Him even as E'noch walked with God. The Father was so pleased that as God and E'noch communed with each other, God just decided to take His boy home to be with Him forever. In another place, we find out that the children of Israel knew the acts of God, but Moses knew his ways. God is relational; we find this in Genesis as He fellowshipped with Adam in the garden. Should it seem strange to us that the Father longs for a people that will love Him, know Him and fellowship with Him? He did not make us robots. He gave us a "free will," so it is up to us whether we want to serve Him or not. God has provided an awesome opportunity for his creation to come into fellowship with Him, by getting to know Him. We go from glory to glory. I believe it will take eternity and going to heaven to learn who our Father is and what He has done for ages to come.

2. Another benefit to prayer is healing and deliverance.

We love to quote the verse in prayer, *"But he was wounded for our transgressions, he was bruised for our iniquities, the* chastisement *of our peace was upon Him, and with His stripes we are healed"* (Isaiah 55:5). One of the names of the Lord is Jehovah-Rapha, which means "the God who heals." Jesus has provided a wonderful benefit in the atonement as our Healer. He not only wants to heal our physical bodies and deliver us from strongholds, but anything that enslaves us from having liberty in Christ. Life will always create opportunities for hurt and wounds to take place. Jesus said offenses must come, but He has given us a wonderful remedy for wholeness. God is a God of restoration and knows how to make all things beautiful in His time. Our Father knows how to heal the brokenhearted, and He is able to give us beauty for ashes. We live in a fallen world and sometimes evil seems to prevail. Life is not perfect and people are not perfect. Therefore, we make mistakes, we hurt and we offend each other all the time. God made us so he understands the feelings of our infirmities. We must take time to cast all our cares upon the Lord and always remember He cares for us.

3. Another benefit to prayer is seeing the faithfulness of God.

As we seek God for deliverance and freedom on behalf of others, the Lord proves Himself strong in breaking the powers of darkness and setting the captives free. The word of God tells us that the weapons of our warfare are not carnal, but mighty through God to the pulling down of strongholds. I have seen God turn things around through intercession time and time again. The scriptures give us great hope as we see how God's people were delivered when they entreated Him through prayer. One favorite story of mine is found in 2 Chronicles 20, which tells us about a great multitude that came against King Jehoshaphat. The scripture further declares that the King feared, and set himself to seek the Lord, and proclaimed a fast throughout all Judah (vs. 3). Sometimes situations and circumstances overwhelm us; but when we set our face to seek the Lord, He is able to grant deliverance. God wants to intervene against the powers that be many times, but it is up to us to turn to Him and take Him at His word.

4. God's unconditional love and forgiveness.

When we mess up or fall short of the grace of God, and we all do, it is a wonderful relief to know He is always ready to forgive and to cleanse us from all unrighteousness. God is never tired or irritated with us for making mistakes. He keeps on forgiving us for our sins and mess-ups. There are many passages in the scriptures, both the Old and New Testaments, which expound on the love of God. One of my favorite verses tells us to *"Love the lord thy God with all our heart, and with all thy soul, and with all thy strength, and with all thy mind; and thy neighbor as thyself"* (Luke 10:27). If God's children could only get a revelation of His unconditional love, we would be a lot better off and have fewer problems and insecurities. I dare to say we should not be so quick to run to other things or people who will not fulfill or satisfy the void that is in our hearts. Only the Holy Spirit can do this work, as we yield to His leading, we will go from glory to glory and strength to strength.

5. Lastly, there are still multitudes not saved.

There are still many nations and people who do not know the Lord Jesus Christ as their redeemer. John 3:16 still speaks volumes if we have an ear to hear, *"For God so loved the world that He gave His only begotten Son, and whosoever believes in Him shall not perish, but have everlasting life."* It grieves the heart of God that multitudes of people are perishing every day. Jesus suffered, died and went to the cross, so we could be redeemed from the hand of the enemy. The word tells us every knee shall bow and every tongue shall confess that He is Lord. So, as we pray and intercede, may we be mindful that it is the goodness of God that brings repentance. God will also empower us by His spirit to come to Him because no man comes on his own. It is the Father's will that fervent intercession, along with the church becoming the salt and the light, reaches every nation and every tongue. It may be someone in our household or an entire nation given to idolatry; but when much prayer goes forth, the powers of darkness are broken and the captives are set free.

Chapter Five: Questions for Reflection

1. Who has been your greatest influence in learning how to pray?

2. Now that you know some of the benefits of prayer, how will you move forward?

3. Are people any different now than the disciples who followed Jesus?

CHAPTER SIX

All Kinds of Prayer

I Timothy 2:1-4 gives a scriptural reference to the different kinds of prayers. Paul is exhorting, Timothy his son, in the faith that supplications, prayers, intercessions, and giving of thanks be made for all men. For kings and for all that are in authority, that we may lead a quiet and peaceful life in all godliness and honesty, for this is good and acceptable in the sight of God our saviour, who will have all men to be saved, and to come to the knowledge of the truth.

Below are various kinds of prayers listed that one can use to define their lives. God is a very creative God and in His wisdom, He has permitted us to come before Him with different kinds of prayers designed to fit the occasion. We will begin expounding on the prayer of thanksgiving.

Thanksgiving and Worship Prayer: The prayer of thanksgiving is self-explanatory. Think about our children or anyone who approaches us. If our little ones come with an attitude of thanksgiving, how much more are we willing to accommodate them and help them with their needs and desires? If we come before the Lord with a genuine need, it is not likely that our request will be denied. It is hard to deny someone with a thankful spirit, and it is the same way with the Father. He says that in everything we are to give thanks, for this is the will of God. In addition, he tells us to be careful for nothing; but in everything, by prayer and supplication with thanksgiving, let your requests be made known unto God (Philippians 4:6). So how do we approach God with a *spirit of thanksgiving*? Well, we just say, "Thank you, Lord." There are so many reasons to give Him thanks. We can thank or praise Him for his goodness, His kindness and his many blessings. We can thank Him for the last thing we asked Him for and He answered. Thanksgiving may include praising Him, singing to Him, and reverencing Him through our worship. This is a time to let God know how much we love and appreciate Him for things He has done. In other words, make a big deal out of praising Him and magnifying His name. We are here to make His name great! Jesus said, "If I be lifted up, I will draw all men to me." With this in mind, make a demand upon yourself to always come before the Lord with praise and thanksgiving. Like David, the sweet psalmist of Israel, we will enter His gates with thanksgiving and His courts with praise.

Warfare Prayer: *"For we wrestle not with flesh and blood, but against principalities, against powers, against the rulers of the darkness of this world, against spiritual wickedness in high places"* (Ephesians 6:12). The Word of God informs us that there are spiritual forces at work opposing us and withstanding us as we take our stand for kingdom purposes. Our Great Intercessor, the Lord Jesus, is seated on the right hand of the Father making intercession for us. He will not leave us alone to fight our battles. God has given us a Helper, the Holy Spirit, who will teach us how to pray as we ought to pray. There have been many times in my life when I did not know how to pray about a situation; but as I began to pray in the spirit, I had great confidence that I was indeed praying for my situation according to God's will. A good thing to remember when interceding for someone is that we are vessels for the Lord to use at that moment. The Spirit of God should be like a conduit flowing through us. As we make ourselves available, God will use us to bring deliverance and salvation to many people. Truly, our Redeemer lives.

Noted author Cindy Jacob expounds in her book, *"Possessing the Gates of the Enemy,"* that prayer is two-fold and it is important to make a distinction between prayer and intercession. She states that many of God's people pray prayers of petition, but never truly learn how to intercede. She says, "True intercession is actually two-fold. One aspect is asking God for divine intervention; the other is destroying the works of Satan" (p. 63). Whether you agree with her definition or not, the fact is we have an enemy that wars against us. So, we must become skilled in fighting the adversary. We must learn how to tear down and root out the plans, schemes and devices of the enemy, regardless, of any opposition we face. Jesus made a profound statement. He said that He came to set the captives free. The Lord Himself is a man of war and His mission is to set people free from demonic strongholds, witchcraft and bondages of every kind. Brethren, we must continue to fight the good fight of faith until the glory of the Lord fills the earth.

Intercessory Prayer: A simple definition of intercessory prayer is coming to God on behalf of another. A more biblical term is called "standing in the gap." God has devised a wonderful strategy to get prayer for people when needed for whatever reason by giving others a burden for them. As we stand before God calling their names and pleading their case like Abraham, we know the Judge of all the earth will do right. C. Peter Wagner's book *"Prayer Shield"* gives a clear definition of the word *intercession*. Wagner says that the term intercession is derived from the Latin "inter" meaning "between" and "cedere" which means, "to go." He states further that intercession is going between or standing in the gap. Through Ezekiel, the prophet, the Lord says, *"And I sought for a man among them, that would make up the hedge, and stand in the gap before for the land, that I should not destroy it; but I found none. Therefore, have I poured out mine indignation upon them; I have consumed them with the fire of my wrath: their own way have I recompensed upon their heads, saith the Lord"* (Ezekiel 22:30-31). This scripture is a clear reference to intercession.

Learning the art of intercession can be an awesome weapon in our arsenal against the enemy. In times like these, the urgency of prayer cannot be emphasized enough. The book of Ezekiel gives a very descriptive picture of God's people going the wrong way and the impending judgment that would follow. It is not the Father's will to pour out His wrath, but He cannot find anyone to stand in the gap. He is willing to be merciful; but without an intercessor to turn things around, He must also do what is just. God is searching for someone to intercede for the sin and idolatry that was destroying His people. We know that God chose Moses to lead the people of Israel out of Egypt's bondage, but many times Moses and Aaron had to fall on their faces before God for the sins of the people and for God's wrath to be overturned. This proves how one person can make a tremendous difference in the lives of others if given to prayer. I cannot emphasize enough how intercession has worked miracles and deliverance in my life. At one time in my life, I was at a hard place in my marriage, but I knew how to get in God's presence and seek His wisdom and guidance. God would say to me time and time again, "Do you trust me?" If I did not have confidence in the Lord to know He would strengthen me in my time of distress, I would have never passed the time of testing and trial I had to endure. Over the years, I have grown in the art of intercession and learning how to stand in the gap for others. Although prayer takes much laboring in the spirit, we learn to birth out destiny and we become joyful in His House of Prayer. I count it an honor and a privilege to partner with God in prayer and you should, too.

Oswald Chambers said it best, "Prayer does not fit us for the greater work: prayer is the greater work."

Prayer of Agreement: The prayer of agreement can be found in Matthew 18:19. Jesus states, *"...that if two of you shall agree on earth as touching anything that they shall ask, it shall be done for them of my Father in heaven."* The word agreement in the Greek means "to be harmonious or symphonize" (*Possessing the gates of the Enemy*, p. 93). Jesus says, *"Where two or three are gathered together in my name, there am I in the midst of them"* (Matthew 18:20). Here, we have a picture of two people partnering together with God, and each other as they agree on their request or petition. It is a powerful thing when two or more believers can agree on the same thing. The prayer of agreement is a perfect opportunity for us to unite our hearts with that of the Father so His will may be done. Many blessings and breakthroughs to prayer can be answered when people come into agreement or have the same mind about something. I might add the prayer of agreement is one of the most powerful ways for married couples to warfare against the enemy. The next time you find yourself in a dilemma, just get another believer to come into agreement with you and watch God bring the breakthrough and the turnaround speedily. Truly, it is good when brethren dwell together in unity.

Persistent Prayer: One way of having persistent faith is "just -Don't Give Up." Say these words out loud, **"I will not give in to discouragement and despair. My God is faithful and He will do what He says He will do."** Go ahead and say those words aloud. Now say them again and then thank the Lord because He will not fail you in your time of need. Jesus is known for His many parables as He expounded to the disciples the mysteries of the kingdom. One such parable can be found in Luke 18:1-8. In this parable, Jesus gives a profound example about being persistent in prayer by saying "men ought always to pray and not faint." In this story, Jesus tells the story of a widow who wanted to be vindicated of her adversary. The parable tells us the judge did not fear God or man, yet he realized the woman was relentless in her petition and would not give up. Even the unjust judge had enough understanding of the power of persistence and granted the woman her request. What victories would be wrought if we would practice the same level of persistence in getting our prayers answered? I believe we would not only get our prayers answered, we would see signs, wonders and miracles. Now, do not get it twisted! God is not an unjust judge like the one in this parable. He is a loving father who wants His children to come to Him with confidence and remind Him boldly of his promises. The Bible speaks of another woman who was persistent in pressing into prayer. Her name is Anna, a prophetess who was about eighty years of age. The Bible tells us this woman departed not from the temple, but served God with fasting and prayers day and night (Luke 2:36-37). What a testimony to the faithfulness of prayer and what God will do if only one person does not become weary in well doing. We may not be called to be an Anna, but there is grace to press in to God for whatever we need. We must not give up or lose heart. God is faithful and He will come at the appointed time.

The Screaming Prayer: There is no biblical definition of a screaming prayer, but I would like to use this example among the many kinds of prayers to make a point. Several psalms admonish us to cry out with a loud voice. So bear with me as I describe a situation that took place several years ago in what I would call my hour of distress. In 2005, my family experienced a house fire and we lost everything, including everything destroyed by the smoke. Thank God for insurance and the church was a tremendous blessing to me, at that time, as the money kept pouring in. The Lord had given me a dream a few days before the fire. I saw myself holding a check for $3,000. That put a big smile on my face and upon awakening; I thanked God for the increase. Nevertheless, the Lord truly does work in ways beyond our comprehension. Isaiah 55:8 says, "For my thoughts are not your thoughts, neither are your ways my ways, sayeth the Lord."

For months, I had been praying for increase and finances, but I never guessed it would happen this way. I had also gotten a prophetic word a few months prior that God was going to give me a new house. **Yeah right!** Nevertheless, the word of the Lord prevails. Well, the house fire was not the only distress in my life. My marital woes increased continually as my husband and I argued about everything from the cat to his behavior. We had a lot going on, and our differences were tearing us apart. Despite my constant warfare, I continued to pray that the Lord would intervene and give me a breakthrough. One Friday evening, just before I was preparing to attend intercessory prayer, I had concluded that I had had enough. My grace to endure his lies and deceit had run out. My husband and I fought once again about his behavior. I felt so helpless, so powerless to do anything and it did not seem God was anywhere around either. As I drove up on the church parking lot, my spirit was heavy and the tears kept falling. Suddenly, I began praying in a way I had never heard myself pray before. I began screaming and saying something like this, "God where are you? Why don't you do something? I have done all I can to make this marriage work and now I just do not know what else to do. Now you said if I call, you would answer. Now do something God - just do something!" I cannot say I had faith that God would do something, but I proceeded to Friday night prayer just hoping I could get through it. The shame of what I had just done was getting the best of me. I guess you could say I felt some kind of way.

To my surprise, God did do something. When I returned home, my husband apologized and said he would try to do better. Well a little change is better than no change. Things slowly began to turn. Do not misunderstand me. I am not advocating screaming our prayers at God to get His attention. I think that particular prayer was birthed out of pain and desperation, but God is still faithful. I have never prayed another screaming prayer. Beloved, whether it is a screaming prayer or a silent whisper, God hears.

Chapter Six: Questions for Reflection

1. What is your favorite kind of prayer?

2. How are you blessing others with your prayers?

3. How has prayer changed your life?

CHAPTER SEVEN

Things that will Hinder Your Prayer Life

Sin is a big hindrance to our prayers being answered and becomes an inroad for the enemy. We as believers must strive to live by the righteousness of Jesus Christ and not by our own works. Romans 6 states a profound question, *"What shall we say then? Shall we continue in sin, that grace may abound?"* When I gave my life to Christ over thirty years ago, there was no place for sin or disobedience to God. Although, I was a babe in Christ, all I wanted to do was please God and do what He told me to do. I was deeply aware that the Almighty God had touched my life and He wanted me all to Himself. He wanted me to love Him with all my heart, my mind and my soul. God wanted me to walk with Him so He could teach me His ways and fill me with His spirit. I have never regretted my decision to give my life over to Jesus. Becoming His disciple and living a life of holiness are my greatest joys. As believers, we must learn to walk in the Spirit and not in the flesh.

The Bible tells us if any man be in Christ he is a new creation, old things are passed away and behold all things become new. As followers of Christ, we learn to walk in the newness of the Spirit in humble dependence upon the power of God not only to save, but also to deliver and put us in right standing with God. Whom the Son sets free is free indeed. As believers, we must have purpose to live a life of purity. Satan will come, but let him find no place in us.

Not being filled with the Spirit

The Holy Spirit was poured out on the day of Pentecost as the Lord had promised, and the disciples in the Upper Room were all filled with the spirit and began to speak in tongues. The gift of tongues is given by the Holy Spirit to all who will ask in faith. This gift will greatly enhance your prayer life and help stir up the gifts that are in you and is a gateway to flowing in the anointing. Jesus said we have not because we ask not. In Acts 19: 2-6, it was here at Ephesus that the apostle Paul asked certain disciples that million-dollar question: "Have you received the Holy Spirit since ye believed?" The disciples replied, "We have not so much as heard whether there be any Holy Ghost." At this time, these followers of Christ were only familiar with the baptism of John. Paul continued to expound to them that the baptism of John was one of repentance. After this, they were baptized in the name of Jesus and as Paul laid hands on them, they all received the Holy Ghost, spoke in tongues and prophesied. This wonderful gift of the Holy Spirit is still available for anyone who will believe and ask in faith, not doubting.

Being too Busy

We all have things on our plate and for the most part, our plate is running over. We only have twenty-four hours in a day, so we all have an equal footing on how much time we have. It is what we do with our time that we must prioritize by doing the things that are needful. Taking time for prayer and communion with God is a must in the lives of believers, so we must be careful to do our due diligence in things that matter. Jesus said man does not live by bread alone, but by every word as it proceeds out of the mouth of God. The psalmist said, "Early will I seek thee." That is another way of saying, "I am putting God first." The scriptures also make reference to Jesus arising at an early hour before His day began to spend time with the Father. Being too busy to spend time with God should never be in competition with any activity in our lives. It is a matter of knowing what is important and making it a priority. There are times I miss that early morning communion with the Lord; but when I do meet with Him, it is oh so precious even though I may still pray before the day is over. Abiding in His presence will saturate us in new and fresh ways in carrying His anointing. Give your schedule and time to the Holy Spirit and trust Him to set things in order.

Strongholds and Generational Curses that need to be Broken

We all have things in our family that need to be broken. It is true that God has saved us with so great a salvation that even the angels desire to look into it. Nevertheless, many times things from our forefathers follow us from generation to generation. These curses and strongholds will often become a stumbling block in our walk of faith. Yes, Jesus paid it all, but we may still need some things broken and put under the blood. For example, a spirit of poverty is keeping you from the blessings and breakthrough that God has promised you. You recall grandma was poor, mama was poor and it seems that every family member you know is struggling financially. You have to borrow every week just to make ends meet and so the spirit of poverty has been passed down to your third generation. What are you going to do? You know this is not the will of God. Beloved, there is a way out! We as believers can claim the promises of God and see change and incredible breakthroughs in our situations that will break the cycle of poverty. As we wait on God to break the spirit of poverty, we can partner with God and do some things. We can tithe faithfully and give God what belongs to Him. We can also sow into the work of God and take our giving to another level. Of course, we take authority over the spirit of poverty and lack through prayer and decrees such as we are the head and not the tail, above and not below, we are blessed coming in and blessed going out. This includes spiritual blessings as well. Overall, I believe God hates poverty, but He is willing to open the windows of heaven and pour out His blessings with the blink of an eye. As T. D. Jakes says, "Can you stand to be blessed?"

Issues of the Heart

Who knew better than David, how the issues of a man's heart must be dealt with as we live this Christian life. David cried out in Psalms 51:10 *"Create in me a clean heart O God; and renew a right spirit within me. Cast me not away from thy presence; and take not thy holy spirit from me."* David had given in to his fleshly desires by committing adultery with another man's wife. After a short period of time, God sent the prophet Nathan to rebuke David and make him aware of God's impending judgment. Someone once said, "Sin will take you further than you want to go, and keep you longer than you want to be kept." Most of us will concur with that statement. Therefore, it is best to tell the truth and shame the devil.

Sin will always grieve the heart of God and open the door for the enemy. Although, God would forgive David, He said the sword would never depart from David's house. As we read the story, we see the sad commentary of what happens in David's household that could have been avoided. David loved his children very much, yet judgment fell on his house and after many years, his kingdom would inevitably be divided and his legacy tarnished. As believers in Christ, we must learn to guard our hearts by keeping it pure and holy and doing those things that please the Lord. It matters little if you are a king ruling nations or a handmaiden who waits on tables. God still looks for the one whose heart is pure.

Lack of Faith or an Unbelieving Spirit

Several years ago, as I walked in the sanctuary praying as I was accustomed to do, the Lord spoke something very profound to me. What He said opened my eyes to something that was enlightening and later shifted things in my prayer life. He said something like this, "O daughter, you are great in prayers, but your faith is weak." I admit up to this point, I had not considered the role of faith in answered prayer. Sadly, I would spend many hours praying for God to do something, but leave out of His presence with very little expectation that He would do it. Have you ever heard the saying, "Houston, we have a problem?" Well it took a minute to even admit that I could be found so lacking in my faith. Needless, to say it was true, so what was I to do? How could I develop my faith and my expectation of God answering all my prayers? Therefore, I repented of my unbelief and asked the Holy Spirit for His help. Then I began to take authority over wavering spirits and anything which would cause me to be double minded. After all, didn't He say, if we come to Him -we must believe that He is and that He is a rewarder of those that diligently seek Him (Hebrews 11:6).

I asked the Lord to lead me and show me how to be a woman of faith. I began to read about people who had great faith in their walk with God. I studied Hebrews 11 and meditated on each one from Abel to Abraham. Why were they known as people of faith and found worthy to be in God's hallmark of faith? Another thing that the Lord pointed out to me in my study was verse 13 which says, *"These all died in faith, not having received the promises, but having seen them afar off, and were persuaded of them, and embraced them, and confessed that they were strangers and pilgrims on the earth"* Wow! Is it possible to have faith and still not receive the promise. I may not have a full revelation on that passage, but the word of God is true, and that is that.

Beloved, the last thing I want is to spend hours praying God's will in prayer, and have my prayers canceled because I don't believe God has heard me. I still have a ways to go in my walk of faith, but like so many that have gone before me my cry is "Lord I believe, but help my unbelief."

Going through a dry season? Don't give up and don't turn back!

One of the wisest men on the face of the earth said, "...to everything there is a season, and a time to every purpose under the heaven" (Ecclesiastes 3:1). It is true that God is with us at all times, for He has promised to never leave us. Regardless of your level of faith or ability to persist or be diligent in your call and devotion to the Lord, there will come a time or a season when it will seem you are going through a dry season. It may look like God has packed up, gone on a long vacation and not said when He would be coming back. In a dry season, you do not feel His presence like you used to and perhaps you have not heard Him speak anything significant to you in months. I have experienced such a time when my spiritual life seemed so mundane and dry that I hardly knew if I still had a relationship with God. I cannot describe anyone else's experience, but I was miserable. I am one who needs to feel His presence and hear His voice. In this parched state, my prayers were reduced to a religious duty and I wanted God to do something, but God did not seem to respond. For instance, I can easily identify with the words of Job. It is not difficult to identify with his plight, as He so eloquently states his condition. As I begin to meditate on the words of Job, I believe I understand what he is feeling and currently experiencing.

"Behold, I go forward, but he is not there; and backward, but I cannot perceive him: On the left and, where he doth work, but I cannot behold him: he hideth himself on the right hand, that I cannot see him: But he knoweth the way that I take: when he hath tried me, I shall come forth as gold." Job 23:8-10

Of course, we know that in the end God delivers Job and blesses him with twice as much as he had before. Satan was granted permission to attack him. God is a God of restoration and according to 1 Peter 5:10, *"But the God of all grace, who hath called us unto his eternal glory by Christ Jesus, after that ye have suffered a while, make you perfect, establish, strengthen, settle you."*

Chapter Seven: Questions for Reflection

1. Which of the topics listed above can you most identify with? Explain.

2. In what way has the Holy Spirit helped you to overcome and break free?

3. How do we remain steadfast in our faith during trying times?

CHAPTER EIGHT

My Call to Prayer

My call to prayer has been one of the greatest blessings on this side of heaven. There was no way for me to know the debt of my call to prayer in those early years. God gently led me and gave me the grace to sit at His feet and learn the things He wanted to teach me. During this season, I was a young Christian and still had much to learn about the art of prayer and intercession. I remember how God would wake me up in the middle of the night or in the early morning hours just to be with Him. I looked forward to my early morning times with the Lord as my love and passion intensified to know Him and do His will. During these times, I did a lot more worshiping and praising God than actual intercession, although, I was faithful to pray for family members and a few church people. God was stirring my heart to pray what was on His heart, and believe me He has a lot of things on His mind for His people to stand in the gap. During these intimate and sweet times of being in His presence, God would also give me worship songs. I was faithful to write them down and eventually teach people some of these songs as He opened the door for me to become a worship leader. My experience of leading worship was also a beautiful season in my life.

My season of leading worship continued for several years; but as the door began to close God began giving me dreams validating this season was shifting, also. During this time, Holy Spirit saturated me with His spirit and His power. God was allowing my roots in Him to go deep as He taught me how to study His word and become sensitive to the prompting of His spirit. I learned to hear His voice with confidence as He began to lead me by His spirit in even the smallest things.

I remember one such occasion while washing dishes. I could hear the soft whisper of the Holy Spirit urging me to pray for a certain person. Well, I had all intentions of praying, but usually I would attend to God's nudging after I completed my dishes. Yes, the Lord allowed me to finish my dishes in that hot, soapy water; but to my surprise, the anointing to intercede had lifted, as I did not respond promptly to the Lord. When I inquired to the Lord about it, He said He was requiring *prompt obedience* because many lives depended on it. Now, I learned my lesson and did not do that again. There is great value in learning to be sensitive to the Holy Spirit. When God speaks to us to do something, all He wants to hear is, "Yes Lord to your will and your way."

Also, one of the desires of my heart was to work at the church. I had been a substitute teacher, but I grew weary of that phase of my life, especially after I gave birth to my youngest daughter Fayth. At this time, I was hoping that the Lord would open a door for me to work at the church in some capacity of worship. However, God answered me but not in a way I expected. One day Pastor Kyle spoke to me and said he had gotten a large amount of money to be used at his discretion. He wanted me to come in for a few hours each day and pray for Him and the needs of the church. Wow! I accepted. Maybe it was not for leading worship, but prayer was the next best thing. Who would not serve a God like this!

God already had me praying for my leaders and the church, so I was already in the will of God concerning prayer. The Lord knew things were tight financially, and He included financial help because I was no longer teaching. In addition to this, my husband began to complain about me not finding a job. But, blessed be my God, who opened a door for me to do what I loved to do and be paid for it. God reminded me of what He did for the mother of Moses.

Take a look at the following passages:

"Then said his sister to Pharaoh's daughter, Shall I go and call to thee a nurse of the Hebrew women, that she may nurse the child for thee? And Pharaoh's daughter said to her 'Go.' And the maid went and called the child's mother. And Pharaoh's daughter said unto her, 'Take this child away, and nurse it for me, and I will give thee thy wages. And the woman took the child, and nursed it" Exodus 2:7-9.

Now I was being paid to do the thing I loved. I was wonderfully blessed by what God was doing, but one day in prayer, I heard the Lord say, "Are you ready to release your Isaac?" The Lord knew I had fallen in love with worship and was not completely ready to release it and move forward. I perceived at this time God was calling me into full-time intercession. I had already sensed the grace for me to sing worship was coming to an end and He just wanted me to be ready.

By this time, I had become much more skilled in intercession and warfare praying, so the anointing to pray was at another level. Although the personal warfare was intense, knowing that God was answering my prayers was a great blessing. Eventually, I did release my Isaac; and shortly after, I took a step of faith. The Lord opened a door for me of full-time Intercessory Ministry, as I became the Head Intercessor for Fresh Anointing House of Worship, Montgomery, Alabama. God is in the business of doing miracles and that is what He did. Is it possible to get a full reward for doing what you love to do? Yes, anything is possible with God, and I am still reaping the benefits of the Lord's favor and blessing. I continue to serve as Head Intercessor under the leadership of Bishop Kyle and Pastor Kemi.

CONCLUSION

Now concerning the things that I have expounded upon, this is the sum of the matter. God has given each of us a measure of grace. This grace is only necessary on this side of heaven. Beloved, we need God's grace to live right, to treat others right and walk in love. We need grace to stay saved and lift up the name of Jesus. We need grace to resist the devil and wage war against the powers of darkness. Finally, we need grace to pray without ceasing. Prayer is a wonderful and powerful tool in the life of a believer. When *prayer is mixed with faith*, these two ingredients become a dynamic explosion to let us know, with the help of God, all things are possible.

Moreover, the Bible gives us numerous accounts in both the Old and New Testaments of men and women who depended upon the faithfulness of God to answer prayer. Well, we cannot find one instance where God failed to come through or disappoint his people when they cried out for His help and intervention. This blessedness of prayer has continued to flow over the years as those who followed Christ continues to call upon the One who is able to do anything but fail. Over the years, I have personally experienced hundreds of answered prayers in my life as well as others. As we learn to rest in the Lord and become familiar with His ways, countless lives will be transformed because we carry the fragrance of Christ. This comes as we abide in His presence. One of my favorite passages that I like to meditate on is Psalm 91, *"He that dwelleth in the secret place of the most High shall abide under the shadow of the Almighty...."* God is looking for those whose hearts will pant after Him. Simeon, a man of great faith, held fast to the promise that he would not see death until his eyes saw Jesus. The prophetess Anna labored in fervent prayer for many years until the Messiah came. Of course, this book would not permit me to name all the ones who labored in prayer as revealed by the scriptures. According to Acts 2, the disciples, along with the women, strained in prayer until the promise in Joel 2:28 was fulfilled on the day of Pentecost. Prayer is one of the pillars that established the early church, and it continues to be a necessary pillar in building God's New

Testament church. There are many other contemporary figures who spent countless hours interceding and praying for God's will to be done. Child of God, the saints of old, like Simeon and Anna, have fulfilled their purpose in praying the will of God. It is up to us now to continue the legacy and pass it on to the next generation. Beloved, it is ordinary people like you and me who God is calling to fulfill the mandate to make His church a House of Prayer. As the Bride of Christ, we must press in with great perseverance to see revival and awakening in the Body of Christ. Nevertheless, we must continue to be faithful as those who have gone before us even though many of them did not inherit the promises. *"And these all, having obtained a good report through faith, received not the promise, God having provided some better thing for you, that they without us should not be made perfect"* (Hebrews 11:39-40).

Pray this prayer with me:

Come Lord Jesus!
We are desperate for You
and all creation is groaning
and waiting on you.

Lord, only you

can satisfy our thirsty souls;
for you, oh God,
have put eternity in our hearts.
Jesus, Your bride awaits!

MODELS OF PRAYER

A Prayer of Thanksgiving

Father, you said in everything to give thanks, for this is the will of God. So thank you for your many blessings that you have poured out upon me. I understand that every good and perfect gift comes from you. Thank you for watching over me, protecting me and covering me with your blood. Thank you, Father that your mercies are new every morning and your faithfulness will never fail. Holy Spirit, remind me not to stress or be anxious for anything, but teach me how to cultivate a heart that is always grateful. In Jesus' name!

Warfare Prayer: Coming Against the Enemy

Heavenly Father, You have given us the keys to the kingdom. You said whatever we bind on earth, you will bind it in heaven and whatever we loose on earth, you will loose it in heaven. Right now Lord, I bind every attack, scheme and plan of the enemy to harm or injure me or my family members in any way. I use the authority you have given me as a child of God, and I trust in your word to deliver me because your word is true and will not return void. Lord, the enemy may come, but let him find nothing in me. I resist him, oppose him and plead the blood against his works. I decree that I am more than a conqueror, and I am anointed to tear down satanic strongholds and do great things for Your Kingdom. Give me the heart of a warrior and make me your battle ax. In Jesus' name!

Intercessory Prayer: Salvation

Father God, you said to come boldly before the throne of Grace to obtain mercy and find help in a time of need. I bring _____ before you. Lord, you said no man can come except he be drawn, so I ask you to draw the heart of _____ closer to you. Open his eyes, Lord, and show him how much he needs you in his life. Remove the spiritual blinders placed on him by the enemy. May you grant to him a spirit of repentance and brokenness that he may turn his life over to you. Lord, you said you know the plans you have for us. They are plans to prosper us and not to harm us, so we may have a hope and a future. So let your will and plan for _____ prevail. Circumcise his heart to love you. Move the stumbling blocks and distractions assigned to get him off focus. Loose a hunger and a desire for righteousness and send spiritual laborers across his path. In Jesus' name!

Prayer of Agreement: Two or More

Lord Jesus, right now, I come into agreement with my brother/sister concerning her finances. According to your word in Matthew 18:19, you said whenever two or more come into agreement you are in the midst. Father, we agree it is your will to bless her finances and prosper her. We agree that every curse of lack and poverty is broken off their life and that they have more than enough to meet their needs. Father, open the windows of heaven and pour out your blessings upon her. Do exceedingly and abundantly above all we can ask. Reveal yourself as Jehovah-Jirreh, the God who will provide. Lord thank you for a turnaround and a breakthrough in their finances. We decree increase and abundance in this season. In Jesus' name!

Prayer of Faith

Holy Spirit, I believe every promise in the word of God is yea and amen. I believe God is able to do what He says He will do. You said if I have faith the size of a grain of mustard seed, I can say to the mountain be thou removed and it would be removed. Lord, increase my faith to believe you and to trust you more. I want to dream big dreams, so help me to take you at your word. Uproot every spirit of wavering that would cause me to doubt your word or be double minded.

Lord, give me the grace to walk by faith and not by sight. In Jesus' name!

ADDITIONAL PRAYERS

Prayer for Purpose

Lord, I make myself available to you. Help me to be your witness for reaching souls. Make me bold and courageous to speak your word and do your will. Fill me with confidence and assurance to be one of your laborers for the end time harvest. Holy Spirit, teach me how to contend for the Gospel because your word is true and every promise is "yes" and "amen." Lord, empower me and anoint me to be a fisher of men, for your kingdom is at hand. In Jesus' name.

Prayer to Stay Focused

Lord, loose a hunger in me to know you, spend time with you and sit at your feet. Lord, I make myself available to you. Teach me your ways and root out anything in my heart that displeases you. Give me greater discernment and wisdom against the strategies of the enemy. Move any distractions in the way. Give me grace to focus on you and to set my affections on things above. Teach me how to lay down my own life and pick up my cross and follow you. Lord, I decree your protection over my life. Be a wall of fire around me, a shield against the enemy. In Jesus' name!

Prayer for Protection

Father, I decree that no weapon formed against me or my family will prosper. You said you will contend with those that contend with me and you will save my children. Your word is true and your promises stand firm. I decree that I am more than a conqueror, and I can do all things through Christ who strengthens me. I believe the Christ is arising within me to step out in faith and believe you for a new level of the supernatural in this season. In Jesus' name!

Prayer for Teaching my Hands to War

Holy Spirit, teach my hands how to war and my fingers how to fight. Lord, give me the strength and wherewithal to be one that enforces the Kingdom. For the weapons of our warfare are not carnal, but mighty through God to the pulling down of strongholds. Lord, I use the authority of your word to pull down, to root out and to make void every operation of witchcraft assigned against me. I bind up word curses that have been spoken against me. I come against generational curses passed through the bloodline for four generations. I close every door to the enemy and cancel every demonic activity working against me or my family to hinder me or hold me back in any way from what God has for me. I plead the blood of Jesus over my family, myself, my destiny and all that pertains to me. I decree that it is well with me, and the good hand of the Lord is with me. I decree that the Lord of Host will fight for me, and He will direct my way for He is a man of war. In Jesus' name!

Prayer for the President of the United States

Lord, I pray for the President of the United States. Your word tells us that first of all, supplications, prayers, intercessions, and giving of thanks, be made for all men. So, I bring Mr. President, his cabinet, his team, his advisors and all the leaders who will speak into his life that you grant them your wisdom and insight to lead this nation. Father, I ask for you to shield and protect him and give your angels charge over him. Holy Spirit, place a hedge of protection around him and his family. I pray that no harm will come to him and that you will keep sickness away from him. I pray for traveling grace and great personal strength to fulfill his assignment in doing your will. Keep your hand upon him and may no weapon formed against him prosper. Give him courage and wisdom to lead this nation, so you may prosper your people; for righteousness exalts a nation, but sin is a reproach to any people.

Lord, bless America. May we truly become one nation under God. In Jesus' name!

Prayer to Overcome Disappointments and Failures

Holy Spirit, heal me from past hurts, disappointments and failures. Lord Jesus, help me to forget of all the times I made mistakes and did not get it right. Forgive me for the times I did not listen to you and did what I wanted to do. For you said whatsoever a man sows that shall he also reap. Lord, I am ready to move on now and fulfill the call on my life. I want to forget the pain of my past and move forward to what is ahead of me. So right now, I loose myself from any unholy connection or any unclean or perverse spirit that will hinder me from following after you. I purpose to live a lifestyle of purity and holiness because my life is not my own, I belong to you. Thank you, Lord, for saving me. Give me an obedient spirit that I may follow you and serve you all my days. In Jesus' name!

Prayer for Singles

Lord, I pray on behalf of every single person to have your delight of glory upon his or her life. I pray that every need to live as a chaste bride here on earth is in total submission to you. Let every single person seek your permissive will to live holy, acceptable, and pleasing to you. Every need and desire for marriage or singleness is "yes" and "amen" in our lives. Let our lives be purpose-driven with favor, destiny, and adoration to walk in faith. In due season, we will reap a plentiful harvest of your greatness and abundance in our obedience to you. Holy Spirit have your way, we need you to consume us with your fire and use us to take dominion of your kingdom. In Jesus' Name! -- Sherry N. King

Prayer for Marriages

Father God, I pray for every married couple across this nation that you have placed together. Let no man put asunder. I pray the power of agreement enables us to walk in unity and communicate with one another as you have unto us. Let our ways please you. Send Angels from every direction to have charge over our families and let your grace abound in our lives. Lord empower us to walk in completion and oneness that exalts you and impacts our families. Allow our lives to be a beacon of light that will be an example to other marriages and those who desire marriage. Bless this union daily. In Jesus' Name! -- Sherry N. King

Prayer for Healing

Thank you Heavenly Father for your promise of healing. According to your word by your stripes, I am healed and made whole. You are still Jehovah Rappha the God who heals. May your healing power saturate us from head to feet. Bring this body into divine alignment, for your promises are true. Thank you Lord for healing me! In Jesus me!

Prayer for Children

Lord, Jesus I know children are precious to you, because every child is a gift from Heaven. Your word declares children are the heritage of the Lord and the fruit of the womb your reward. Jesus save our children/child. Deliver them from the snare of the enemy. Break every stronghold in their lives and turn their captivity. Cover them in your blood and give your angels charge over them. Thank you Lord, for you have power to save and to deliver. In Jesus' Name!

Prayer for the Body of Christ

Lord Jesus, I bring your people before you, for you alone are God. Glory, wisdom, and honor belongs to you. Father, I believe all things are possible and the prayer you prayed in John 17 will happen just as you said. We will be one in

Spirit, soul, and body. Jesus pour out great love and unity upon your church. Give us the same care for one another. Help us to see one another through your eyes. Lord, we are your people called by your name. Let your will be done. Let your kingdom come. In Jesus' Name!

Prayer for Walking in the Spirit

Holy Spirit, teach me how to walk by the Spirit and not the flesh. Teach me how to walk by faith and not by sight. I do not want to make decisions based on my emotions or what I feel, but what I hear you saying according to your word. You said if I acknowledge you, you will direct me in all my ways. Lord, I loose myself from all pride, anger, jealousy, envy and bitterness. Furthermore, I forgive those who have wronged me or offended me in any way. I choose the way of love and forgiveness. Give me the grace and strength to do it your way. In Jesus' name

BIBLIOGRAPHY

Bickle, Mike. (nd). Prayer Quotes. Retrieved on January 10, 2017 https://markbroadbent.org/prayer-quotes/

Bright, Walter. (2015). Seven Days without Prayer makes one Weak. Retrieved on January 10, 2017 https://walterbright.org/2015/01/08/7-days-without-prayer-makes-1-weak/

Bounds, E. M. (2014). How to Pray, Prayer Quotes, Prayers, The Necessity of Prayer, Why We Need to Pray. Retrieved on January 10, 2017 https://prayforrevival.wordpress.com/2014/03/20/e-m-bounds-god-shapes-the-world-by-prayer/

Chadwick, Samuel (2017). Inspirational Quotes. Goodreads Inc. retrieved on January 10, 2017 https://www.goodreads.com/quotes/288521-there-is-no-power-like-that-of-prevailing-prayer—

Chambers, Oswald. (nd). Key of the Greater Work. My Utmost for His Highest. Retrieved on January 10, 2017 https://utmost.org/the-key-of-the-greater-work/

Jacobs, Cindy (2000). Possessing the Gates of the Enemy: A Training Manual for Militant Intercession. Revised Edition by Chosen Books

Jakes, T. D. (2000). Can You Stand to be Blessed? Treasure House.

Murdoch, Norman. (2017). Sayings of William Booth. Christianity Today.org retrieved on January 2017 http://www.christianitytoday.com/history/issues/issue-26/sayings-of-william-booth.html

TO THE READER

I decree that the Lord God is with you and that His plan and purpose for your life is unfolding even as you are reading this book. I decree your time with God will never be the same. I decree that your prayers and intercession will affect multitudes and nations as you learn to enforce His kingdom. This is a new season for you. Believe God for doors to be opened and the favor of God will rest upon you. God has enlisted you in His army of prayer, and you will do much harm to the powers of darkness and the workers of iniquity. You are God's champion, His battle ax and His bride. Your prayer life will shift and things will be broken off you as God takes you higher in His spirit. I decree that right now, this moment. Every stronghold and plan of the enemy to hold you back will be rooted out, and you will go forth in the power and anointing of the One who is all powerful. The works of the enemy have been broken and God will teach your hands to war. Child of God, you were created unto God for good works. You will and you shall fulfill your divine purpose. You have much work to do, so rise up and let not your hands be slack - for your work shall be rewarded. Blessings to you!

BIOGRAPHY OF THE AUTHOR

Pastor Diane has been a faithful follower of Jesus Christ for more than thirty years. In 1977, she graduated from Talladega College with a B.A. in English. Pastor Diane serves as the Head Intercessor of Fresh Anointing House of Worship, founded by Bishop Kyle Searcy. She was ordained in 2010 as a Pastor of the ministry and has assisted with pastoral duties. She has also served on ministries such as intercession, deliverance, praise and worship, and WIMI - Women In Ministry International founded by Pastor Kemi Searcy. Pastor Henderson also teaches classes about dream interpretation, intercession and prophetic ministry.

Pastor Diane has been married for over thirty years and enjoys spending time with her family. She has five children and several grandchildren. Henderson's greatest passion is to see God's people grow into spiritual maturity and fulfill their prophetic destinies. She has labored through prayer and intercession for many years for the body of Christ to be awakened to the call to pray and a greater revelation of the holiness of God.

Pastor Diane is also the author of *"Burning Hearts"* a twenty-one-day devotional designed to help new believers grow in their intimacy of God and become passionate about the bridegroom.